Stories from Islam

Daud and Jalut

Ziya Us Salam

Om KIDZ
An imprint of Om Books International

Salman had come home from school. Putting his school bag down, he rushed to his grandmother, Rasheeda. "Grandma! Today, we read the story of David and Goliath. Goliath was so big! Do you know their story, Grandma?" Salman asked his grandmother excitedly.

"First change your clothes and have lunch. Then we will sit and talk about David and Goliath, all right?" Rasheeda ruffled her grandson's hair.

Salman changed his clothes and finished his lunch quickly.

"Prophet Daud, mentioned in the Quran, and David, mentioned in the Bible, are in fact, the same person. Daud was both a prophet and a messenger," explained Rasheeda.

"What is the difference between a prophet and a messenger, Grandma?" Salman asked.

“A prophet,” Rasheeda began, “is one who has received the Revelation from Allah, but who is not commanded to spread it, but to follow it himself. A messenger is one who receives the Revelation of a law from Allah, and is called upon to spread it among the common people. Thus, every messenger is a prophet, but every prophet is not a messenger. There are more prophets than messengers.

"Daud was both a messenger and a prophet. He was given a revelation from Allah, a message, to add to the Taurah, which was revealed to Prophet Musa. This revelation was called the Zabur. It is also called the Psalms by our Christian and Jewish friends. Jalut is the Quranic name of Goliath."

"But, Prophet Daud defeated Jalut, didn't he?" Salman wanted to confirm the story he had studied in school.

"Right, Salman, he did. But you must understand that all divine stories have a message. Daud was shorter than Jalut, who was very tall and strong. Daud won because he was intelligent. It is important to rely on your brain rather than your physical strength.

"In the Quran we read about Talut, the king of Israel. He was not accepted by the rich men in Israel. They thought that since they had more wealth, they were more worthy of being a king. But Allah gave Talut knowledge and wisdom.

“One day, Talut set out with his army to meet Jalut in battle. As his army was about to cross a river, he ordered his men not to drink from the river.

"Most of his soldiers did not obey his command. After crossing the river, these soldiers felt that since they were a much smaller army in comparison with Jalut's, they would lose the battle.

"Those who had obeyed Talut were confident that Allah would help them. Many battles had been won by smaller armies, they told themselves. After saying their prayers, they faced Jalut in battle. Prophet Daud killed Jalut with the permission of Allah.

“He became the king of the Tribe of Israel. Under his rule, all the Tribes of Israel became united once again. The story of Prophet Daud is mentioned in the Quran in Surah Baqarah.”

"Thank you, Grandma! I will surely read this story in the Quran," Salman promised, and rushed to his friends.